Before The Rainbow

Emmanuel Fru Doh

Langaa Research & Publishing CIG
Mankon, Bamenda

Publisher:
Langaa RPCIG
Langaa Research & Publishing Common Initiative Group
P.O. Box 902 Mankon
Bamenda
North West Region
Cameroon
Langaagrp@gmail.com
www.langaa-rpcig.net

Distributed in and outside N. America by African Books Collective
orders@africanbookscollective.com
www.africanbookcollective.com

ISBN: 9956-791-83-0

Dedication

For John Lenjo
Intellectual extraordinaire,
With fruits unharvested,
That your name may never die.

To God Almighty Be Praise And Glory

Table of Contents

Preface

Nobody can honestly sing about the beauty of the world or true love on an empty stomach or with Achebe's proverbial home ablaze. It is with this in mind that I lament the fact that there is smoke still bellowing from the crevices of our united abode, in spite of the time and energy that has already gone into this, prompted by political guile and deceit. Hence, in the heart of this circus of a union, we have had to wade the political tide with daring moves by Bamenda and other Cameroonian cities like Bafoussam, Douala, and Kumba in an attempt to bring about change. As we failed in the effort, *Not Yet Damascus* confirmed the recalcitrance of the leader who will not approach Damascus to be baptized and converted by the veritable doctrine of true love for one's fatherland and fellow man. This would have ushered in the end of this persecution of a citizenry transformed into wretches by a blighted leadership and hence the repentant Saul.

As his leadership continued trampling on everything, we took refuge in the brave culture of scholarship represented by the University of Ibadan, of long ago, by celebrating a veritable establishment in the hope that our academic and political leaders may learn; it failed: old habits die hard. They decided to remain political minions, academic dwarfs, confirming themselves shadows of all that they pretend or claim to be. Even then, time never stopped moving, and so if events have failed to oust the octogenarian through political strategy, the time has come when his going out is a must: age will oust him whether he likes it or not. Hence this volume

Before the Rainbow, since one can only hope his demise will bring about efforts towards a period of true love and peace.

Someday then, I hope to sing more songs with more soothing concerns, but not yet, not with our home still ablaze, consumed by the fires of inequality before the flag, corruption, exploitation, abuse, victimization, divide and rule and so on. Before such a panorama, how can one sing of something else without biting one's tongue as one's thoughts stray away onto painful battles awaiting one at the end of love songs? How can we tell of joy when our neighbour's pension is yet to come years after he went on retirement? How can we honestly describe the beauty of the sky and the sweet smell of flowers when national heroes die in poverty only to be posthumously "insulted" with worthless decorations that bring nothing to their families or their memories? True love is the fruit of a mind largely satisfied, a mind essentially at ease, one that can, confident of an existing national support system, soar high into the skies without rainclouds of doubts and the fear of an existing bazaar of a nation to bring about bumpy rides. Such an atmosphere, like the rainbow, will only come after the storm, which somehow must come to pass, sooner or later.

We Must Talk

We must talk! We must talk
To usher in the rainbow:
The tables have tilted with
So many promises broken
And our protestations ignored;
We must talk.

We must talk, we must talk
If the rainbow will mean anything:
Our resources have been plundered without gain
Our landscape blatantly ignored
Our children and our goals slighted.
We must talk.

We must talk, we must talk, for
Our bodies and minds have been scarred
By gendarmerie hooliganism,
Our minds distorted by divide and rule
With suspicion rife amidst us.
We must talk.

We must talk, we must talk:
It is the path to peace and love;
Dialoguing breeds understanding.
Who is afraid to talk but the thief,
Thieves of our constitution.
We must talk.

We must talk, we must talk
If we must go past this bazaar

If we must in place a structure
And our country managed as ours
Instead of reporting in colonial palaces
We must talk.

We must talk, we must talk
To know what our sons and daughters
Want, to help them reconnect, if need be,
To apologize here and there for hurts
Revealed by the lips of history
We must talk.

We must talk, we must talk
If we must be one again
And feel that we truly belong
Instead of this division we wade in
While a few thrive over the majority
We must talk.

We must talk, we must talk,
Then the colours of the rainbow
Would be brighter and string together
Our thoughts and wishes with the
Chord of love and nationhood
We must talk.

We must talk, we must talk
That this nation must grow
We must talk that this nation may
Emerge with a positive vision
Unlike the dead we are without a purpose
We must talk; indeed we must!

Our Heads of States

You were head of state when I was born!
The tedious investigative years of
Infancy and toddling have comeand gone,
Even the elementary is disappearing
In the horizon, and I have your name
To continue to memorize as head of state.
The years of understanding in secondary,
High school, and now the University
Have left their bitter toll on my mind,
Yet you leech to that office
Twisting the rules of the game to
Legitimize your stay as silver and gold
Buy more days. Today I carry my son
And stare into his blank gaze and
There is your name still being blared forth
As head of state; alas your citizens
No longer smile but turn aside, your
Once appealing appellation now a scourge.
It is an illusion to buy time. Seeyour scalp,
Once overwhelmed by rich black strands,
Now still black? Even a child can tell,
Can tell how much attention you give it
To fool yourself about your exuberance.
See the muscles of your visage, once firm
And spelling handsomeness now sagging,
Jaws turning into jowls like a bulldog.
Time is power; only the fool tries to corrupt it.
I hear the bells tolling: Etoudi soon must
Be evacuated and accountability rendered
Where cash holds no tender:

Ahidjo! *Monsieur*!
Mobutu! *Oui Monsieur*!
Mbongo! *Present*!
Boigny! *Je suis là*.
Ha-ha-ha-ha-ha-ha!

Merging Realms

(For John Lenjo)

Genius un-plucked, voracious reader who
Relished the use of effective diction and
Trembled at the efficacy of expressions;
In the battles of the hour, blessed, cursed,
You trod a path known to few, peopled by
Characters, gorgons experienced by you alone.
In the whirlwind of the hour
Your soul torn between
Realms, the physical and the supernatural,
I witnessed you fighting in control to stay.
You denounced visitors from strange
Realms violating your existence.
These encounters, in brief spouts,
Leaving outsiders perplexed as
In and out of battle you surged;
The way of the world. Brave warrior,
I bear you witness of cascading danger
When both worlds embrace in a body
When both worlds clash in a mind
Only God's name and His mercy redeems
At this point: no medication, none,
Not even the whips of the witch-doctor.
In the end of it all, you will find peace,
I know my friend, for I remember that faith.

Lone Warrior
(For Albert Womah Mukong)

And now Mukong, at the
Threshold of your plight,
Battle against kleptocrats,
Battle against treasonable felons,
The picture is beginning to be clear:
The meaning of your struggles
The value of your sacrifice.

In the face of our betrayal
You alone stood your ground
Refusing a part of it to be
As peers pitched in with Iscariot
A piece of the silver to taste.
In jail you rot, ignored by
Compatriots, friends even, yet
Alone in your convictions you
Stood; time proved you right.
You may not have won completely
Lone warrior, but your effort
Proclaimed your roots – a people
Who know their taste. Rest that
Body even as echoes of your
Struggles continue resounding from
The man-made walls surrounding
Our hijacked existence.

With The Internet

In this age and hour, I see
And sense the cracks on the walls
Of our values pitted against dirt
With debauchery legalized and celebrated
In infernal Sabbaths before the eyes of children;
These early cracks on our walls,
The walls of our ways, once guarded
By family pride, the pride of the village.
In this platform that belongs to nobody,
Where all can be seen and practiced unrestrained,
I fear for tomorrow the cultural
Bastards these will grow to become.
Slowly but surely like the growth of a pregnancy,
Slowly but surely like the arrival of darkness
This electronic clash, today's colonialism,
Is too much a price to pay? Where is our
Respect for birth-orders and broken calabashes
Whenbefore my eyes eaglets grow in defiance
Of the bald eagle, and fragile cubs poised in insubordination
To black-maned lions. Today we stand in defiance
Of our identity in adoration of another's vile ways
Blind to our noble values in the face of waste.
This internet thing.

It's All A Game

They came stealthily,
Brandishing the bible
And preaching against my
Grandfather having many wives;
Today the same people
Are telling me it is alright
For me, a man, to marry
Mammy Anye's son.
Where now is the hell that
Was to swallow my grandfather?
If no be craze this
Then nawetin be craze?
Wuna tell me. This people
No get shame. Small time
Dem go stand for television
And fight make woman marry dog
Because na dem right to do
Anything wey dem want do.
Craze peoplecallam say freedom.

True Victim

Woe is one pioneering these consanguineous
Cantankerous brood. A king trailed by
His queens, but you, this deficient driblet
Trailing, I recognize not.
I have heard of the bad seed,
You are more like the bad egg.
Everything about you reeks,
Your actions, sitting in judgment.
You stand at the spot marking time,
But like a commanding officer, you speak
Dishing out orders, commands and conditions.
Your actions like a fire truck
Announce your deeds and approach
Only for you to forage in the cascading waves,
Grabbing straws of victims for your ranting;
Refusing to come to terms with your
Stringed blunders and like Peter,
Rush to the betrayed in quest of pardon.
I see you as a veritable stallion, riding high
In your pride, but in its wake the fall.
You heed nobody, hence you surprise even
Yourself; this waste.

None is there for you to blame:
When the tunes were being played
For you in counseling, you danced but
To your baseless dreams
Even as the hours ticked by.
Finally even the tortoise was
At the finish line, yet you dined

On your ego, your pride, your recalcitrance
And now you forage in the annals of time
Like a human tornado attempting to seek
Havoc and earn pity.
We had proofed our homes and all
Long ago, your storms are sterile.
We had wept for all long ago, our sorrow
Like the desert drained our tears.
Now we have none to share as you come to;
I hear the bridegroom approaching.
You must today fulfill yesterday's obligation.

Sing my name, chant it, damn it;
You bother me not. Your created tales
Placate only base buds like yours
Hungering for idle gossips. Great minds judge
For themselves rather than follow
Reptilian tongues lacing tasty
Snippets of Scheherazade's brew.

Academic Titles

Academic titles are not pacifiers
But honoured time-tested decors,
Crowns, tassels, and fleeces
Generated by gladiatorial academic feats
Marked by years of hard work,
Discipline, patience, dedication and excellence
Within academic amphitheaters of sorts.
I am disgusted when Ambition toys with them.

Stones from a Glass House

So my father passed on,
And then you, supposedly my father,
Have continued clawing at, stabbing
In a worthless fight for dusty articles.
And in the process
You have spoken of my sister's
Scandal, a leopard free of spots?
Or else bear not fruits
That they may not be blighted
By the hand of fate, triggered
By your mockery of another's cross.
To live in a glass house and throw stones?
There is no better mark of folly.
A woman who is fertile
Ridicules not the deeds
Of another's children;
Nature, sometimes, has a
Few expensive jokes up its sleeves.

In This Confusion

In this confusion
The blood of the innocent bathe the
Streets, while heartless leaders
Soar above, unrepresentative guests.

In this confusion
The blood of the hungry and destitute,
True national victims, colour our
Pavements scrubbed off by champagne
Bubbles and the expensive fumes
Coughed forth by parliamentarian
Rides in dislocating luxury.

In this confusion
Idiotic soldiers kill their compatriots
Valuing the ammunitions more
Than God's sons and daughters
Whom they slaughter in cold blood,
Leaving wives without husbands
Children without parents:
Then anger and bitterness thrives
As hatred is sown amongst a people

In this confusion
I have seen the worth of human
Life dwindle as soldiers and the police
Take civilian lives without a thought.
Crisis broods armed with alien
Automatic weapons pillage, rape and plunder
Even with the thousands of bribe sniffing

Uniformed men and women I see by day.

In this confusion
All is lost as might has become
Right in our bloodied existence
With its quest for vile trash,
Ephemeral Midas,
With God banished from our nations
And our ancestors held at bay
Without those frequent invitations
By palm-wined invocations.

In this confusion,
See what we have become.

The Tongue

To look a person in the eyes
Smile in his face
And then pierce a dagger from
Behind into his heart:
That is what slandering does.
You nurse and eliminate his fears,
Trash his concerns as trite
And so earn his complete trust
Only to turn around and misrepresent
Him to others, usually strangers
To the victim who otherwise would
Hold him in awe. They pass on
Your vile stories about an innocent soul,
They pass on your lies about a trusting
Friend, brother, cousin, fellow man,
On and on the damage of his portrait
Spirals even to age-groups below his.
Alas by God's grace your audience,
After all your calumny, meet your victim,
Only to discover a soul far removed
From your horrid tales even as your
True character comes to the fore.
It took years, but the Master
Vindicated him. Slander is murder
And so God rejuvenates the victim's
Portrait for God alone accords
And only He can take life without
Consequences. Learn then your lips
Together to keep if your goal is slander.
Above all learn humility

The much you think you know
Is nothing in nature's sandy shores
Of wisdom. Learn humility
For even your person is naught
In the aisle of men. Always
A far better there is in everything.
The wise, even with Wisdom for a friend,
Strive like the Master before Pilate to be.

The Smith
(For Bill F. Ndi)

I love the new faces
At the start of each semester.
I enjoy the different attitudes too,
Knowing how hard I must work
To break them to this new setting.
My voice like hammer on ananvil
As to work I set, chiseling here and there:
Encouraging now, threatening then,
Penalizing after all. Hurt, disappointment
And sometimes anger at my effort.
Then realization dawns, humility sets in,
The will to learn soars: now they
Know they don't know – reason to be
In my class – and acknowledgement
Is not a sign of weakness.
The sound of my hammer all round
The clock, falling in shape, and
Then they must depart; I must let go.
Like ladies and gentlemen, some
Thank me for all I have done,
Others walk away assuming they paid for
My dedication. I will miss them for a while.
Even as I struggle with the names;
It's a new class; the cycle with the smith.

The Stage

Quietly it crept in
Stealthily the props fell in place.
Once towering bituminous shafts fading
And shrinking, lightening up sporadically
Ensuring visibility, thinning in numbers
And clearing up even, opening up cranial
Islands of scanty that boldly announce the stage
With stiffness and blunt cracking
For scenic exeunt even as
Once vivacious actors now plod
About in their roles.
A pill here and there to lubricate
To relax and slow down
Even as the stage conveys its
Message of what next.
Like the xylophonist's final mournful note
And she who keens her explicit ablation.

Mungwin

Your flight is a death sentence,
Suicidal ride on airwaves,
Wingless effort; to powerful
Bulbs, light in the tunnel,
The nocturnal sky late
In the year.

Down you soar into the light,
You damned heavenly manna,
Into man's fatal embrace:
The wingless phase, the
Oily phase in saucepan
Stir-fried in your own fat.

Without any regrets we eat,
We sell, we eat, only to
Lament the passing days
As the arrival of *mungwin*
Dwindles and so our
Hoarded supplies. Never mind
Next year will do.

When A Mountain Speaks

Like a victim in the distance
Taking all the abuse from
Man – harvesting wood and
Building farms and houses.
From nature; the cold, the
Wind, the clouds, the rain,
What noble essence!
Until in response it pukes
Divulging steamy larva
Clearing a path from the summit
To the shore - Mount Fako.

Changing Guards

The tin roofs are rusty red
Thinly carpeted by layers of crusty dust
That for months have been provoked
Into an uprising only to settle back
Down in disgust at the nonchalance of
Others. Then the winds would tear across
Powerful but premature tornadoes
Spiraling upwards, high into the air
Spinning and lifting dust particles
Paper, pieces of cloth, scores of
Polythene bags through its vortex,
A witch at work - children - as
They see people running away afraid
Of being sucked in and upwards.
Then the rain drops, first in sluggish isolation
Like a reluctant lover; then the drops increase
In number into a shower and more
Sometimes. After a few blinks
The eyelids of dust and rain clouds
Clear up and stare, letting in
The bright and soothing rays of the sun
That espy the young dragonflies
Wafting themselves unsteadily on fledgling wings
Like drunks, mesmerized by the new season.

Lament Of A *Bushfaller**

I am away from you
Not because I like it.
I am away from you
Because the music I danced
To was changing,
The rhythms unstable,
A hole in the palace drum.

I am away from you to search
For steadier rhythms,
Yours my dear I failed to change
And my life in danger from
Acolytes of the palace musician.

See then my departure darling
As clawing at straws for survival
Instead of a betrayal
Instead of failing love.

Remember I have dipped
In your waters and know the depths
To my new shores a stranger you are.
Judge me not in the distance
Then, my rhythms are new and
Strange, so anew I begin.
Consider me not changed
But a dancer with alien steps
To which I must yield
Or else perish again.

From the distance my new
Rhythms are pleasant to the ears
Come into the dance and see
For yourself: The steps are imposed;
Nothing spontaneous, a
Stranger to yourself you become
Again clutching at straws
In the name of this dream.
More often than not it is
A *bushfaller's* nightmare.
The hours you must put in,
The Western Union calls
From the native shores
And you dare not fail.

You my friend must know
How hard for me the one to be
Doing all to stay connected
While all you do is nag,
"Now a bushfaller he has
Forgotten me, our good days."

I have not!
For you I yearn every day Fatherland,
For the once calm rhythms at home
I long, but how could I stay?
The old man needs a cane
A role I will otherwise not fulfill.

Outside bushfallism:
See me not as estranged
By choice – the music, the music

Of bushfallism. To listen to
Is not to know
To dance to it is to discover
The truth – a challenge!!!

*In Cameroon today, a "bushfaller" is anyone who, for whatever reason, has abandoned the national territory to reside, temporarily or on a permanent basis, beyond the continent of Africa, especially in the West.

Mr. Henry Von René

What *acarè* did to
My people, how can I forget?
Some came as traders, others
Came claiming in search of
Friendship to be. Metusa
Welcomed them; they bought,
Bathed, ate, and slept with us.
When they left, our homes were
In shambles; everything upside down.
Our leaders they had killed
Or on exile, to foreign lands,
Banished. Our palates transformed
Our fields now looked different:
We farm for their industries
Instead of our bellies as before.
They slept with our queens and
Denied it, until *Abaŋa* emerged.
They beat out elders before our very eyes
And made them work for free –
The French especially – and
Carried away our produce
For free, setting up
Banks and businesses that
Fed their metropolis with the products
Of our labour. They even claimed to be
Better, but all they did showed
Them petty thieves from our vineyard.
They claimed they were better
And many of our people believed,
Yet until today Mr. Henry has

Only two eyes and a long nose,
Von has only two hands and two legs
René has a stomach like mine,
With a treasury River Congo keeps afloat,
Yet without a doubt
All three have shrunken grub between
Their thighs, yet claim to be better.
They drum and sing about what
They do, but like co-wives
Push under the earth what we do.
These people have no shame:
They have no respect for anything
Except money; this is all they know.

Beware Africa

Beware Africa
Lest tomorrow you say
I did naught about it,
Lest you lament after
The die is cast
That you were not told.
Instead of standing your ground
Like David, in mud you chose to plod
After Goliath because his armor glitters
Yours are noble ways,
By time tested,
Yours are noble values
Bequeathed thee by generations
Of sages with a profound sense
Of what is right and wrong.

Beware Africa of these new doctrines
Of today that pretend to be best.
Beware of nonsense fed you
In the name of correctness:
How correct is it for a mother
To kill her own child?
How valuable are fertilizers,
Chemicals that have left our soils barren?
Is it equality for a child
To disrespect his parents?
And now men sleep with men
And women with women
Something my dad will not do,
Something my mom will not do.

Beware Africa
Of strange ways on strange waves.
Yours are ways that the gods,
Even their great book acknowledges.
Beware Africa!

Colonial Mentality

See that policeman at attention when
That white messenger came in,
He was relaxed and smiled stupidly
When Foncha and Endeley showed up.

See that soldier,
He carried that white clerk's
Bags for him; he kicked that
Black woman engineer's bags
Aside and threatened to whip her.

See that doctor smiling like an idiot
In front of that white woman
Picking up her purse from the floor for her,
He would not look at my sick mother
Waiting hours already for his arrival.

See that teacher,
He beat Anye until he peed
In his pants; he wiped the seat
For that white student who came
Late to sit down without addressing
His tardiness.
See that judge,
He sentenced Mbangwi to six
Months hard labor; he sent Underwood
Home.The prisons here are too
Dirty for him in spite of his
Being the brain and Mbangwi an accomplice.

See that secretary,
She told Jean Escargot
Who had just shown up,
"The Minister will see you now,"
But ignored Etoundi who had
Been waiting for hours.

See that customs officer, my classmate
Smiling stupidly and helping
Foxwood with his unsearched bags
Loaded with contraband,
He rips open Namondo's bag
Only to find gifts for her children.
The white smuggler laughs and drives off.

See our mentality?
You treat him like a lord in Africa
He treats you like shit in Europe
He gains twice – Colonial mentality

Mrs. Bigman

You who knew not what tomorrow
Had in store, who had nothing for dinner,
Today you spin the car-key holder
About your knuckles – indicative!

You who interacted with the broke
And dreamt of hope for tomorrow
With your likes, now a snub, and
Will not make time to talk to the needy?

You who loafed about in need
And prayed that God will come to your help?
Now you look low on the needy,
Poor hard working people?

Because today you are spouse to
A big man? Man's memory, how short!
You've forgotten the poor who fed you,
The hardworking on whose shoulders you
Cried out your plight?

Mrs. Bigman, beware of fate and time
These jokers in the card-pack of time
Deal strange hands. Remember them today
That they may remember you tomorrow.

Big Man Palaver

My people sometimes sound
Like an empty can.
They sometimes sound like a shell
On the ground after the shot:
Nobody wants to serve
Even in rags and worn out shoes,
They love to play big man.

The D.O. sits like a small god
Behind an oversized table
With the moron's head of state
Smiling down at him from above his head
As if to say well done.
The D.O. will ignore Cameroonians
Waiting for his signature
And not feel a quailing.

The Gendarme whistles a
Passenger car to stop but
Sits by his roadside office and
Waits for the rights-less driver to
Run to him with bribe in his documents.

The doctor looks on with disgust
As the old lady reels in pain
Only to condescend an I.V. glucose
To a diabetic.

The priest is too busy for
My *mea culpa*, but drives

Around doing nothing like
Our civil servants before *midi*.

Mammy Goat-pepper-soup refuses
To sell to her patron,
But smiles moronically as she
Dishes goat meat pepper-soup for
The Lebanese store owner.

The young cashier even
Refuses to offer the customer
A smile: she is now too much
For him – this wretch whose
Money pays her meager salary;
She is now a whole cashier.

A collection of empty cans
Who think to serve is trite.
All they do is pose around
From dawn to dusk instead of
Feeling good about being of service.
Everybody thinks he or she is everything
The other needs for survival;
This Big Man Palaver.

My people think to be of service
Is a sign of failure, even those
With degrees and trainings that
Should be humble from learning small gods
Have become. We need each other
The thumb may be thicker, it
Is no more useful than the pinky.

In serving there is dignity
And vainness in lording it;
The humble that serve win after all.
So did the Christ.

This Other Invasion

Long before my eyes my ears could see
Our ways were like the rules of nature,
Firmly in place, nothing could move.
Then the huge fish with towering fins puked
On our shores – began the journey to
Decadence.

Before you answered *Ngui's* call from
Beyond the clouds *Teuhn*Njoya,
You thought you had seen it all; before
Your call Kamah you lamented the
Trends you saw, not knowing mere
Scouts they were.

I wonder what you would have done
Had *Ngui* permitted you to see today,
Had *Nyikob* blessed you with a few more
Rains Kamah, I wonder what your
Lamentations would have sounded like,
As you question today's offspring's origins.

Now Angwi sits, in the midst of men,
Elders, hanging her legs miles apart like a man,
Without decorum, nor respect.
Nfor walked past me yesterday,
Looking at me straight in the eyes,
But will not greet.
Fonyuy spat back words into his father's
Mouth – they are now age mates.
Today's red feathers no more value seem

To possess – elders now tell lies, stealing
From the palace even.
I have seen palm-wine rejected for
Liquid in a bottle, and watched
Ngwe eat *achu* with a spoon as men
Look on with nothing to say.

African Woman

Your beauty's beyond description
With lovely curves that beckon,
Your *lolo* vibrating to your strides
Forever tantalizing the environment.
Nature's gift to society you are,
For we see and get, true to your man,
Without decadent additives here and there
Traps to male longing: your lips so full
Without botulinumous milliliters.

African woman,
Your dreams are different, your goals unique:
The family. Learn not from guinea pigs
That have gone wild thinking carnal pleasures,
Freedom, and equality, with God shelved
To be summoned on their terms.

African woman,
Until you care less about your family
Then begin learning from tastelessly high cultures
In the name of civilization, bothering yourself
About equality with a gender that is only a rival.

African woman,
You are the wife, the mother the core of the family,
Of society, your presence sooths the household,
Calming the lion and the cubs,
Why would you become something
Else that results in destruction and pain?

African woman,
Begin thinking for yourself and beware of alien
Words that taste like honey and sound like music
But lures society to the grave. To them suicide
Means nothing, to us it is taboo.

Mother of the universe!

You Are Just another Human

So much time has come and gone
And still I muse at your behavior:
To condemn without hearing the
"Accused" out? And to claim we
Had been what we were.

After this Odyssey
On me imposed by man
Through which I plodded.
My life became a lonely cell
With metaphysical bars restraining,
Victim of charity,
Victim of humility.

Thoughts of friends like you
Gave me hope and the will
To live. My prayers have
Ripped open holes in the walls
Of my cage—mental, emotion, and physical,
Letting me out again to smile,

In apprehension though.
To you my friend, I rushed
Excited your intellectual depths
My plight will fathom and with
Understanding, how I imagined
With teary eyes this "prodigal" you
Will embrace and celebrate

My journey back from the dead

Free at last from Meduza's serpentine
Claws of exploitation and torture.
Yet, when I stretched out my hands
From beneath the stygian deep
You pulled back without any care,
Baptizing my effort welcome but belated.

And I am left hanging, betrayed where I
Trusted, even as I wonder at such a disposition
Where before I saw beauty, intelligence
And what I took for genuine concern.
Indeed life is an intricate mesh
Weaving to sometimes bizarre patterns,
Time, emotions, and experiences.
I have learned and will continue to
In my endeavor human kind to understand.
The lawn is green, I will not let
A browning patch destroy that belief.

Chances!

When a person spends all his time
To make you look bad and
Out of place on God's earth,

When a people spend so much
Of their resources to make you
Look low here on God's earth

They assemble foul names and
Send them your way, call
Their crimes yours and jail
You for it, here on God's earth.

They'd rather you were dead
Than alive, and for no just reason,
Your image and character they
Assassinate, here on God's earth.

They retell and rewrite history
To favor their ways
Ridiculing yours for reasons
Unknown, here on God's earth.

They sleep with your men and women
And try to deny it, but for
The mulatto, and smile with you
Only in private, here on God's earth.

Chances are you're black.

Fon of Fons in Bamenda

The sirens on numerous state cycles
Uniformed officers in their best and numbers,
Some reeking oflast night's alcohol
The festive huza for the New Deal prince.
Like a queen termite surrounded; overwhelmed
He babbles a few words about blessings.

Distinguished traditional leaders like puppies
Betray tradition; shaking hands here and there.
To weather the rising storm, halt the questioning
Glances, declared a fledgling in statecraft
Fon-of-Fons and cooked him done.
These gamblers, toying with our roots for
Worthless recognition: you are the ones that
Wished him long years, judging wine
From the looks of the Calabash.

News of a Colleague's Death

So many waste time hurting others,
They know you not but judge you;
They only hear of you and damn you;
This waste of time is madness.

You hate for no reason and slander
Unprovoked, and in the madness of the hour
Missing out on God's message to you
Through His messenger – His handiwork.

Then you hear death whispering, calling
And another journey abruptly ends
But not before regrets, even as
Simple souls celebrate life.

Keep your doors open that you
May see others smiling,
Your windows ajar that you
May not miss the laughter.

At least once a day remind yourself
Of this pending journey – talk to the Father
So He may prepare you well
For the journey that must come.

This Burden

The sun will rise and the
Day and her events roll on
With that simplistic, that deceptive
Routine, with the impression that
All is well, as things ought to be.
Alas behind certain names
Lie incredible forces at work,
Laying trees on innocent shoulders
The path of life making thorny,
Erstwhile simple and successful
Steps belabored with loaded sighs.
Forge on if you can, lending
A hand here and there if you can;
Never another damn or ridicule.
These battles are mostly personal,
They are mostly private.

The Girl from Port Harcourt

In the layers of years piled on
I see your gentle smile, and radiant beauty,
I hear that voice of power and authority,
Yet you too were only human,
Wanting to be held
Thirsting to be loved
With a smile that radiated confidence
That body gentle, feminine curves, with
That grip so firm and engaging.
Beyond that, your mind was sharp,
Your dialectical engagements charming.
To be beautiful and intelligent,
Shy yet confident, gentle yet poised
How so long since those years
Of love and affection, ONE.

The Dance of Life

How my mind clings to yesterday
The songs to which I listened and danced.
How my body clings to yesterday,
The men and women I knew,
The boys and girls I loved,
How my soul clings to yesterday.
Yet all about it boils down to hurt
The joyful hurt of nostalgia for
The things and people I miss,
Some of whom have gone ahead.
How my body clings to yesterday.
Yet, on, time marches and my days
Remain numbered. I too must go someday.
Even though I hear it is best as
Time becomes the moment – yesterday and today.
Yet as my soul longs to move on
My body clings to yesterday.
The dance of life.

AIDS

The things you've done to me,
Scarred my hide, brutalized
My psyche, cheated me of love,
Denied me rhythms unheard
Of with each death at your
Hands. Do you know how much
I prized the father of Afrobeat?
Do you know how much
I cherished Luambo
The guitar maestro with
Songs and rhythms from Africa's
Ripples? See those scholars
Dying, see those parents
Leaving behind orphans
Transforming death into a game for
The young, which only the old
Before indulged in. Now
They blame us, blame our
Animals and our 'bush-beef'!
What power and having the
Means can do. I weep!

Presi-Who?

To them who have presidents for leaders,
They are choices of the populace supposedly;
To be they are said to have their people at heart
Not so with Africa's, not so at all.
Not with our Fons, Chiefs, Oba's and all
Relegated to the background by modern kelptocrats
Who think naught of their citizens but their families;
With fourth and fifth generation bank accounts
Overseas, their nations brandishing SOS flags.
Thieves for leaders, Lucifer's ultimate barbecue.

Being Of Service

When shall we enjoy
The joys of serving?
When shall we serve
All who come our way
With a smile at least.

Is it that we've always
Been down there and so insecure
That all we want
Is lord and oppress others
Given the slightest chance?

Why are we nice
Kind and friendly
Until we are in power, in control?
And then we want it all,
Even the people to walk on?

May be why some say power corrupts
But those are the vain and haughty
The humble given power, serve!
They are in it for the good of all.
Mandela, Nyerere, Sankara!

Profaning the Rainbow

I miss those days when I held a
Dear friend's hand in true friendship
And it did not matter even if he were a man.

I miss those days when I could hold
And hug a child like a true parent
Without sensing those eyes on me,
With thoughts racing.

I miss those days when mankind was
Humble and the fear of the Lord, the
Northern Star, in all that was said and done.

I miss those days when a smile was a
Smile indeed and came straight from the heart
Not snarls baring hypocritical fangs;

I miss those days when I knew the
Definition of simple words like 'love' and 'marriage'
Without the need to be politically correct.

What a mess we have become,
Hurt God but be politically correct,
Even as we march down the drain.

Strange Notes

The xylophone sounds nothing like a piano
The *ndenge** sounds in its own unique way
But like hyenas in the path of blood
Yapping along like morons,
Like vultures in the path of death
Swishing airborne to the scene.
My people drop all in their hands
To inherit alien values and ways
That shame our grandparents in their graves.
Now murder is no longer taboo
Rape is creeping in without anger
Disrespect smiled upon as being civilized
So too are bedmates now mixed up
As deviants come out of their closets of shame,
And some are calling for redefinition
And constitutional rights. Like raindrops
After a tornado, see my people too
Beginning to acquire and emerge from "closets?"
Where is the culture of shame and pride
That used to be a part of our values?
Where is that need to protect,
To protect the integrity of the family name?
Wake up my people and be yourselves:
Because a vulture eats cadavers
So must a dove?
Because a hyena scavenges
It ought not tooblige the lion.

The Mind

The mind is a vast mesh
Of avenues, streets, and alleys
Some our consciousness
Visit on an hourly basis or more;
There are others
Pray never to visit
That you may not degenerate
Into something else,
According yourself a worrisome identity:
Psychopath, mentally ill, schizophrenic.
Praise God and stay in check.

Reminiscing

A view in retrospect,
A look back in time and space,
Hindsight, always revealing,
Always beautiful even with
A few blemishes that yield wisdom.
How beautiful are the flowers
How touching those hours
Up and down the valley of travails
After all now I can only smile
And nod back at the beauty of all,
Of mistakes even, and lessons learnt.

Lucifer's Priestess

To sit, talk, drink, and laugh
The barometre of happiness – misleading?
How wrong!

In the midst of woes
That could bend iron bars
Woes that led others to
An early grave – suicide –yes I ate
And talked, drank, laughed,
And even danced.

But the unseen burden
Gored at the core
Leaving me frightened, sick,
Terribly anxious.Yet
The days rolled on
With me wearing a smiling mask.
And so the meaning of
Viciousness, a part of it
Somehow, I now understand.
For no reason other than
Because I have the power
I can do whatever
To another of God's creatures.

Servant of Gahanna
To plant your bloody curse
On me – an innocent son,
Stealing the best years of my life:
In a daze I lived, for naught

But the want of my sweat,
My hard earned money.

How true the words of the
Master? You and your
Hellish legion battered
Mind and body, the soul
Beyond your ugly reach.
To think how once I revered you,
Loved you like a very mother
And respected you more than your very own
Brood, my reward a bloody encounter with
Your hellish crew by day and night.

The cross won:
The Christ, the Virgin,
Saints Joseph, Jude, Pio,
Michael the Archangel
And so forward I forged
Abandoned by friends misleadingly
Traumatized by my supposedly newfound
Bushfaller mentality even as
My life on the line hung as
I tangoed with death;

What man can do to man!
But Mary, You the Undoer of knots,
Mother you freed me and set
To work in the Master's vineyard;
Holy indeed is His name, and You
Forever shall be called Blessed.

Our Tomorrow

For going against the regime,
The price was costly: hands, eyes, lives,
But on we forged.
I found out not all fought
Others looked on from
The distance and went on with their lives.
Yet true gladiators, we encountered bullets,
Grenades, with our wills for better days.

The price was high indeed:
State of emergency, abusive
Soldiers abandoned by the
Government to rot –
All we had, nothing more
Given my people, others
Rewarded for not fighting
Against the corrupt regime.

We forged on bravely,
The true warriors we are.
They said we brought it on ourselves.
What betrayal: The rising gas prices,
Rising tuition, falling health standards
Capsized salaries our lot alone?

When we abandoned ship
For fruity shores
They blamed us for abandoning
A national cause,
A cause for which we had been

Fighting alone—remember?
This confusion, this apathy!
My people wake up – a
Broom is stronger than one broom stick.
It is our tomorrow, not mine alone,
That is at stake here.

A Solitary Prayer

Listen to our musicians
Lament in their songs,
Hear our scholars
Plead and wail in their works.
Hear them cajole, yet
Those jackals in power
They care not for our lot,
Alienating hats in hand
They roam foreign lands
Patriotic themes on their lips
Begging for money.
The yields from our land they stash
Away, and then beg only to stash
Elsewhere. Like Christ, my people,
The owner of the wealth,
Are presented as beggars.
But Lord you promised us
Rulers after your own heart,
If not now then when Father?
See your children rot alive,
Their wealth dumped abroad
By pilferers at the helm.
Must we all perish first Lord?
Then who shall shout out your
To you, your name in gratitude?
Thy ways are strange, even then
Thy hour, the best. Come!
Come Father and rescue your children.

In Our Midst

My people are different
And with hearts of gold.
Your nose could be pointed,
Or like the beak of an eagle,
Or plain flat like a valley bed
We do not notice.
Your hue yellow, pink,
Black or a combination,
We do not notice.
To us, there is a stranger
In our midst and we
Serve him the best we can,
Serve her the best we can.
We encourage you into our nooks
And cranny, not bar your way
In our midst pretending friendship.
Africa's hospitality!

God Is With Us

(For Reverend Emmanuel Taboh Asongwe)

Is it in our names "God is with us"
Or in the will of God that these
Blows we must receive, our way of the Cross?
Some souls by God chosen to share in His passion?
Else how do I explain the demise of a beloved
Daughter even before she could see the fourth moon?
The hurt you felt, but for the support of family: your
Wife and children!

You were just beginning to breathe again,
Accepting your fate, when like a blazing meteor
The blow landed on earth's crust:
Like child, like mother, transforming you
Into an undertaker gain, this time with a title,
Widower. How you must have been shattered
At the fall of darkness in your household.

The years have come and gone
We are apart, forced by the will to survive
Even as we hurt and hurt. I trust you must have
Turned to the Master and like Job declaring the creed:
The Master giveth, the Master has taken.
Those lines are naught pitted against the pain,
The experience. Yet time has elapsed; it is
Way passed noon, with darkness fading into
Strands of light, wisdom announcing the approaching
Hour, gladiator, when from daughter and wife....

ET Rev! I salute you brother. It is I

Emmanuel Fru Doh, acknowledging your loss,
Acknowledging your pain. Time has passed
And I thought someday the meaning would
Dawn on me,
I still cannot fathom!
I still cannot fathom!